Great Moments in

Olympic
SNOWBOARDING

By Brian Howell

SportsZone

An Imprint of Abdo Publishing
www.abdopublishing.com

www.abdopublishing.com

Published by Abdo Publishing, a division of ABDO, PO Box 398166, Minneapolis, Minnesota 55439. Copyright © 2015 by Abdo Consulting Group, Inc. International copyrights reserved in all countries. No part of this book may be reproduced in any form without written permission from the publisher. SportsZone™ is a trademark and logo of Abdo Publishing.

Printed in the United States of America, North Mankato, Minnesota
042014
092014

Cover Photo: Mark J. Terrill/AP Images
Interior Photos: Mark J. Terrill/AP Images, 1; Bela Szandelszky/AP Images, 6–7; Kyodo/AP Images, 9; The Canadian Press/Sean Kilpatrick/AP Images, 13; Robert F. Bukaty/AP Images, 14–15, 19; Paul Sutton/Duomo/Corbis, 20–21; Douglas C. Pizac/AP Images, 23, 33; Tom Hanson/AP Images, 25; Duomo/Corbis, 27; Laura Rauch/AP Images, 28–29, 30; Lionel Cironneau/AP Images, 34–35, 37; Frank Gunn/AP Images, 39; Jae C. Hong/AP Images, 40–41; Sean Kilpatrick/AP Images, 45; Press Association/AP Images, 46–47; Rex Features/AP Images/AP Images, 50; Andy Wong/AP Images, 53, 54–55; Valdrin Xhemaj/epa/Corbis, 59

Editor: Chrös McDougall
Series Designer: Craig Hinton

Library of Congress Control Number: 2014932863

Cataloging-in-Publication Data
Howell, Brian.
 Great moments in Olympic snowboarding / Brian Howell.
  p. cm. -- (Great moments in Olympic sports)
Includes bibliographical references and index.
ISBN 978-1-62403-398-8
1. Snowboarding--Juvenile literature. 2. Winter Olympics--Juvenile literature.   I. Title.
796.93--dc23
                                                          2014932863

Contents

Introduction

Nobody knows for sure when snowboarding was invented. The sport that combines elements of Alpine skiing, surfing, and skateboarding first gained popularity during the 1960s and 1970s. A spike in popularity during the 1980s helped make snowboarding a mainstream sport by the early 1990s.

Snowboarding eventually became popular around the world. That led the International Olympic Committee (IOC) to add the sport to the Olympic Winter Games. Snowboarding made its Olympic debut at the 1998 Winter Games in Nagano, Japan.

Halfpipe is the only Olympic snowboarding event that has been around from the start. Halfpipe snowboarders perform tricks on a giant, U-shaped course with tall, vertical walls. In 2002, parallel giant slalom replaced giant slalom. That event involves two boarders racing side-by-side while going through gates. Snowboard cross made its Olympic debut four years later. It puts a pack of boarders on the mountain together. They race to the bottom, going over obstacles and jumps along the way.

Two more events were added to the program at the 2014 Winter Games. Parallel slalom is similar to parallel giant slalom. However, the gates are closer together. Slopestyle features one boarder at a time. He or she goes down a hill that features obstacles, such as rails and jumps. Like in halfpipe, judges determine the best performances.

Vancouver 2010
SHAUN WHITE'S RIDE

Shaun White already had the gold medal in the bag before his final run on the halfpipe at the 2010 Olympic Winter Games in Vancouver, Canada. His score from the first run remained the best after all the other riders took their second runs. So the 23-year-old White could have skipped his final run altogether. At the top of the mountain, he made his plan with US snowboarding coach Bud Keene.

"What do you want to do?" Keene asked.

Shaun White flies through the air during the halfpipe finals at the 2010 Olympic Winter Games in Vancouver, Canada.

"I don't know, man. Ride down the middle?" White responded.

"No. Have some fun," Keene said.

"Drop a double Mc?" White said.

"Yeah, drop a double Mc at the end," Keene said with a smile.

White then dropped into the halfpipe. What followed was one of the most sensational victory laps in the history of sports. White was flawless as he began his run. As usual, he flew higher in the air than anybody else on each pass. The big air gave White speed going into his final jump. He crouched down as he approached the lip of the halfpipe. Then he took off.

Moments later, the crowd erupted. White triumphantly raised his arms. He had done it. He landed the move he invented—the double McTwist 1260. That difficult trick requires two flips and three and a half spins in midair.

"I don't think I've crashed as much in the last couple of years as I have this season learning it," he said before the Olympics.

White said the double McTwist 1260 was the most dangerous and difficult move he had ever tried. Yet, on that night, he landed it nearly to perfection.

"I wanted a victory lap that would be remembered. I achieved that," he said.

He certainly did. He scored 48.4 points on that run. It was the highest score ever awarded in the history of the Olympic Winter Games.

A Snowboarding Star

White was already a star before the 2010 Winter Olympics began. He burst onto the scene at the Winter X Games in 2002. As a 15-year-old, White won a pair of silver medals in the superpipe and slopestyle competitions. White missed out on a spot in that year's Olympics. But his star was clearly on the rise.

The 2006 Winter Games were in Turin, Italy. By then, White had won six gold medals at the Winter X Games. But he truly became a household name in Turin. Nicknamed the "Flying Tomato" because of his long, curly, red hair, the 19-year-old White took home the gold medal in the halfpipe competition.

Like in Vancouver, White had the gold medal wrapped up before his final run. Decked out in an all-white suit and an American flag bandana covering his mouth, White dazzled fans with 1080-degree spins in his first run. Nobody came within two points of his 46.8 score.

White performed a couple of jumps during his second run. But he coasted into the finish line with his right arm raised in victory.

Legend Growing

The 2006 Olympics confirmed what snowboarding fans already knew: White was the best around. Outside of the Winter Games, he dominated the Winter X Games in both superpipe and slopestyle. He also won two X Games gold medals in skateboarding. But it was White's performance in Vancouver that made him a legend.

The sport had grown a lot since its Olympic debut in 1998. The tricks were much more difficult and the athletes were better. But White still came into the Winter Games as the heavy favorite. And he left being

International Breakout

Halfpipe snowboarding debuted in the Olympic Winter Games in 1998. From 2002 to 2010, Team USA men were dominant. They had won three consecutive gold medals. In fact, US men had won seven of the nine total medals awarded from 2002 to 2010. However, Team USA was shut out at the 2014 Winter Games in Sochi, Russia. Switzerland's Iouri Podladtchikov, known as "iPod," captured the gold medal. He landed his signature move, called the YOLO flip, during his winning run. The YOLO flip includes two flips and two 360-degree turns. A pair of Japanese teenagers—15-year-old Ayumu Hirano and 18-year-old Taku Hiraoka—won the silver and bronze medals, respectively.

compared to all-time greats such as basketball's Michael Jordan and golf's Tiger Woods. All three dominated their respective sports.

White proved his dominance over and over again in Vancouver. He scored 45.8 points on his opening run in the qualifying round. That score would have been good enough to win the gold medal. Yet White was even better in the finals. On his opening run, he scored 46.8 points. That gave him a commanding lead going into the second run. The other riders tried their best to beat White. But nobody really came close. Finland's Peetu Piiroinen had a good second run. He scored 45.0 points. But it wasn't nearly good enough to beat White.

White Out

Shaun White entered the 2014 Winter Games again as the favorite. He had won the previous two Olympic gold medals. Plus, he had 18 total Winter X Games medals in snowboarding (13 gold, three silver, and two bronze). Instead, White struggled at the Winter Games in Sochi, Russia. First, he dropped out of the slopestyle competition to focus on the halfpipe. Halfpipe scores were now out of 100 points instead of 50. White had a great first run in halfpipe qualifying, scoring 95.75 points. That was the best run of the entire event. But qualifying scores don't carry over to the finals. In the finals, White fell on his first run. Then he could only manage a score of 90.25 on his second run, when he couldn't land his main trick. He finished fourth. "I'm disappointed," he said. "I hate the fact I nailed it in practice, but it happens. It's hard to be consistent."

Shaun White celebrates in 2010 after defending his Olympic gold medal in halfpipe.

White put an exclamation point on the competition with his spectacular final run. He was nervous about falling if he tried the double McTwist 1260 in the first round. But he had nothing to lose in the second. And White made it look easy. In fact, he made the entire competition look easy. Three of his four runs were better than anything any other athlete produced in Vancouver.

"It's impossible to beat Shaun unless he falls," Piiroinen said.

White didn't fall in Vancouver. Instead, he rose to the occasion and walked away as a winner—again.

Nagano 1998
OLYMPIC DEBUT

S kiing has been a fixture at the Winter Olympics from the beginning. Nordic skiing was part of the first Winter Games in 1924. The first Olympic Alpine skiing races were held in 1936.

Snowboarders became a more common sight on the slopes during the 1970s and 1980s. At first, many skiers disliked snowboarders. They viewed snowboarding as a sport for rebellious youths who followed their own set of rules. In fact, for years many ski resorts banned snowboarding. In turn, many snowboarders were

Germany's Nicola Thost performs a trick on her way to winning the women's halfpipe gold medal at the 1998 Olympic Winter Games in Nagano, Japan.

wary of skiers, too. But snowboarders were happy to be outsiders in the skiing community.

As time went on, however, more and more "mainstream" people caught on to snowboarding. The image of the sport began to change as more people realized that snowboarding is actually pretty fun. In 1993, there were roughly 1 million snowboarders in the United States. Two years later, that number had doubled. During the winter of 2012–13, there were almost as many snowboarders in the United States (7.35 million) as skiers (8.24 million).

The reputation of snowboarding changed so much that the IOC could no longer ignore it. In December of 1995, the IOC added snowboarding as a medal sport for the 1998 Olympic Winter Games in Nagano, Japan.

Showing They Belong

Whether people liked it or not, snowboarding hit the grand stage in February 1998. The members of Team USA were thrilled to be part of a new adventure for their sport.

"It's just amazing how it's grown," US snowboarder Shannon Dunn said in 1998. "I can't believe it, and nobody who's been in the sport very long can believe it. When I started, you would know everyone who snowboarded. It's almost like we created what it is."

In some ways, snowboarding lived up to its reputation in Nagano. The best snowboarders in the world brought their own style to the Games. They brought their own language. And they brought their own swagger.

"They're totally new to the Olympics," wrote Michael Wilbon of *The Washington Post*. "They look different, they sound different, they are different."

Snowboarding had its share of controversy during its Olympic debut. Some members of the US team refused to wear team uniforms to public events. Canada's Ross Rebagliati won the first gold medal in Olympic snowboarding history. But he later tested positive for marijuana. Rebagliati was briefly stripped of his gold medal. However, the decision was reversed and he was allowed to keep it.

As for the actual competition, poor weather was a factor during the 1998 Games. The US team was favored to win medals in the giant slalom.

Halfpipe Champions

Halfpipe is the one snowboarding event that has been featured in every Olympics since 1998. Gian Simmen of Switzerland was the first gold-medal winner in the men's halfpipe. Judges gave him a total score of 85.2 points for his two runs. Germany's Nicola Thost scored 74.6 to win the first Olympic gold medal in women's halfpipe.

Instead, the men and women were both shut out. Nevertheless, there was a sense of pride for some of the athletes because they were on an international stage. American Sondra Van Ert went to Nagano for a medal but came up short. She was twelfth in the giant slalom, but left with a smile anyway.

"There's nothing I would treasure more than a gold medal at the Olympics, but I've got a lot to treasure just being here," she said. "It's the neatest thing to ever happen to me in life, being part of this."

Rain made the halfpipe competitions more difficult on the final day. The athletes managed to get through it, though. They put on a show for the fans. Americans would go on to dominate the halfpipe in future Winter Games. In Nagano, US athletes Ross Powers and Shannon Dunn each settled for bronze medals.

The First Gold Medalist

Canada's Ross Rebagliati will always be known as the first Olympic gold medalist in snowboarding. He won the giant slalom event on February 8, 1998. Snow and fog moved into the area during the competition. Still, Rebagliati finished with a great time of 2 minutes, 3.96 seconds. He barely edged Italy's Thomas Prugger, who finished in 2:03.98. Switzerland's Ueli Kestenholz won the bronze. The next day, France's Karine Ruby won the first women's gold in giant slalom. Germany's Heidi Renoth won silver and Austria's Brigitte Koeck won bronze.

Canada's Ross Rebagliati competes in the men's giant slalom event at the 1998 Olympic Winter Games. With his win, he became the first Olympic gold medalist in snowboarding.

Despite a few bumps in the road, the 1998 Olympics proved to be a milestone for snowboarding. The sport, still relatively new, gained more worldwide attention than ever before. Yes, snowboarding—and its athletes—were different, but they were accepted.

"We have been on this crazy quest for legitimacy for so long," US halfpipe snowboarder Todd Richards said. "The Olympics are going to bring a legitimacy into this sport like no one can comprehend."

Salt Lake City 2002
CLARK MAKES HISTORY

It was February 10, 2002. Kelly Clark stood at the top of the chute waiting for the signal to start her final run. A crowd of more than 16,000 people was on hand in Park City, Utah. They yelled and cheered as Clark began gliding down the snow.

During the next 30 seconds, the US snowboarder put on a masterful show for the home crowd. Zigzagging her way down the halfpipe course, she soared high above the walls of the pipe. She got more air than

American Kelly Clark performs a trick during the women's halfpipe at the 2002 Olympic Winter Games in Salt Lake City, Utah.

anyone else in the competition. She performed sensational tricks in midair that wowed the crowd.

Through it all, Clark wore headphones. A Blink-182 song rang in her ears. As loud as the song was, though, Clark could still hear the crowd as she performed.

"The crowd was going so wild, I could hear them over the headphones," she said.

In the halfpipe competition, athletes are judged on their style as well as their technique. Clark's technique was nearly flawless. She also won style points for flying higher than any of her competitors above the 14-foot (4.3-m) walls. Clark's run also included one spectacular jump, a 720-degree spin that capped her ride.

A Bright Star

Australia's Torah Bright made history for her country at the 2010 Olympic Winter Games in Vancouver, Canada. Bright won the gold medal in the women's halfpipe. Through the 2014 Games, Bright's gold was one of just five gold medals ever won by her country in Winter Olympics history. "We're not known for our winters," Bright said. "We do have snow, but we're known for our white sand beaches and our waves."

"I figured I had second place wrapped up, so I had to go for it," Clark said of her big jump. "I knew I would regret it if I didn't."

Clark's final score was 47.9 points. It was more than enough to win the gold medal. France's Doriane Vidal scored 43.0 to claim the silver medal. Clark's was the first gold medal for the United States at the 2002 Olympic Winter Games in Salt Lake City. More important, it was the United States' first Olympic gold medal in snowboarding. Although just 18 years old, Clark became an instant star.

"I wouldn't have thought in a hundred years that I'd be here," the Mount Snow, Vermont, native said. "I really didn't think anything of making it [to the Olympics] until last season."

Clark had to battle through a bit of pain to get her win. A bruised tailbone three days before the finals caused her to miss a full day of

Shannon Dunn

In 2002, Kelly Clark won the first Olympic snowboarding gold medal for the United States. Shannon Dunn made history of her own four years earlier. During the 1998 Winter Games in Nagano, Japan, Dunn won the bronze medal in the women's halfpipe. It was the first Olympic medal for a US woman in snowboarding.

ALT LAKE 2002

Kelly Clark performs a grab during the halfpipe competition at the 2002 Olympic Winter Games.

training. "I was pretty sore, but I had so much adrenaline today, I didn't feel much of anything," she said.

A Snowboarding Champion

Clark's victory was a landmark event for Olympic snowboarding, especially in the United States. The Winter Games in Salt Lake City marked just the second time that snowboarding had been included in the Olympics. There were some people who still weren't sure if the IOC had made the right choice by adding the sport four years earlier. Yet, on that picture-perfect day in Utah, Clark put on a show that was very much worthy of the Olympics.

"Snowboarders have their reputations, but my doing this, especially in the US, says a lot," Clark said. "Maybe it will shine a light on snowboarding, and people will look at it in a different way."

Clark went on to have a remarkable career in snowboarding. She also competed in the 2006, 2010, and 2014 Olympics. She won bronze medals at the 2010 Winter Games in Vancouver, Canada, and the 2014 Winter Games in Sochi, Russia.

Clark was still snowboarding through 2014. Through that season, she was a nine-time gold medalist in the Winter X Games and had more than 60 victories worldwide. That was more than any other male or female snowboarder. Plus, Clark was a pioneer. In 2011, she became the first woman to perform a 1080-degree turn in competition. A 1080 requires three full rotations in the air.

Clark became a hero in the snowboarding community. She even made her mark off the snow when, in 2010, she started the Kelly Clark Foundation. The foundation was designed to raise money to help young athletes and disadvantaged youth. No question, Clark is a legend in the sport. But her gold-medal performance in 2002 was the greatest and most memorable event of her career.

Salt Lake City 2002
TEAM USA GOES 1–2–3

K elly Clark became the first US snowboarder to win an Olympic gold medal on February 10, 2002. One day later, the men took their turn on the halfpipe.

"Just watching her yesterday kind of psyched us up," American Ross Powers said.

The US men went into the 2002 Olympic Winter Games in Salt Lake City, Utah, expecting to do well. What they did during the halfpipe competition was special, though. Powers won the gold medal, Danny Kass won the silver medal, and J. J. Thomas won the bronze.

Team USA's Ross Powers competes in the men's halfpipe finals at the 2002 Olympic Winter Games in Salt Lake City, Utah.

Ross Powers flies high through the air during the 2002 Olympic halfpipe competition.

By winning gold, silver, and bronze, Team USA became the first country to sweep all of the Olympic snowboarding medals in one event. Through 2014, Team USA remained the only country to do so. Also, it was the first US sweep of any Winter Olympic event since the men's figure skating team did so in 1956.

"Snowboarding was started in the USA and there are so many good snowboarders in the USA, and I guess we've kind of been leading the way, whether it's been in the halfpipe or in the videos," Powers said.

Powers came into the competition as one of the favorites for the gold medal. He didn't disappoint. The 1998 bronze medalist was spectacular during the 2002 Games. He dazzled the crowd throughout his gold-medal-winning run. He had back-to-back McTwists. Then he threw in a Cab Cork-720. Powers scored 46.1 points on his winning run.

"I just dropped in and tried to get as much speed as I could," said Powers, who celebrated his twenty-third birthday the day before the competition. "I did a method air, which is a backside air, and then a frontside air. Those are probably some of the biggest airs I've ever done in a halfpipe, if not the biggest."

Snowboard Stars

Powers grew up as a skier in Vermont. He got his first snowboard at age seven. However, he had to share the board with his brother. Soon, though, it became clear that his brother preferred skiing.

"I kind of took over the board," Powers said.

Seeing Silver

US snowboarder Danny Kass won the silver medal in 2002. Four years later, he came back and did it again. Kass threw down an impressive run that netted a score of 44.0 points out of 50. Team USA nearly had another 1–2–3 sweep in 2006. American Shaun White took home the gold. However, Finland's Markku Koski spoiled the party. Koski won the bronze. He was barely ahead of American Mason Aguirre, who was fourth. Four years later, Team USA dominated again. White won another gold, while Scotty Lago took the bronze. It was the first Olympic medal for Lago.

By the time he was eight years old, Powers was turning heads with his skills on a board. He won a senior national title at the age of 16 and the 1998 Olympic bronze medal at 19.

Kass was just 19 years old during the 2002 Winter Games. Known as a very technical rider, Kass came into the Olympics as a favorite to win. He had taken home the gold in the event at the 2001 Winter X Games. At the Olympic Winter Games, Kass's silver-medal run included an inverted rodeo 720. That move has been called the Kasserole. He posted an impressive score of 42.5 points.

Thomas was pretty good, too. He scored 42.1 points to win the bronze medal. Another US rider, Tommy Czeschin, came into the Games as a favorite to win a medal. He even sat in third place after the first run in the finals. However, Czeschin ended up finishing sixth.

"I just had fun on that second run," Thomas said. "I watched these guys do it and I just followed up."

In the end, it was a historic podium celebration. Powers, Kass, and Thomas stood on the podium together.

"I'm really happy to be part of the United States sweep and to be on the podium with J. J. and Ross," Kass said.

From left, Danny Kass (silver), Ross Powers (gold), and J. J. Thomas (bronze) swept the men's halfpipe medals at the 2002 Olympic Winter Games.

For Powers, it was the second time in his life that he had stood on the podium. But four years earlier, he listened to the Swiss national anthem. This time, the three Americans stood with their arms around each other as they listened to "The Star Spangled Banner." And they did it in front of their home crowd in Utah.

"I couldn't ask for anything more," Powers said. "It is the best birthday present ever. These guys [being] beside me is also huge. Today was just the perfect day, awesome pipe, and everything worked out."

5

Turin 2006
TETER SHINES

H annah Teter stood at the starting line waiting
for her turn to race in the 2006 Olympic Winter
Games. The 19-year-old first-time Olympian chatted with
her coach. She danced a bit. And then as her name was
announced over the public address system, she raised
her arms as the crowd in Turin, Italy, cheered for her.

Seconds later, with the fans roaring, Teter exploded
from the start line and attacked the halfpipe course in
front of her. During the next 30 seconds, Teter dazzled
the crowd with incredible twists and flips and an

US snowboarder Hannah Teter competes in the women's halfpipe at
the 2006 Olympic Winter Games in Turin, Italy.

awesome amount of amplitude. The Belmont, Vermont, native made sure it was memorable.

Her run was highlighted by a 900-degree spin (two and a half rotations) that she executed perfectly. Teter wowed the fans and impressed the judges. As soon as she finished, Teter and her teammates knew it was a special ride.

"I'm super stoked," she said.

Adding to Teter's great moment was the fact that teammate Gretchen Bleiler took the silver medal. Kelly Clark, the 2002 gold medalist, finished fourth. Clark might have won the gold—or at least some medal—had it not been for a fall during her final run. Clark attempted a difficult frontside 900 but came up short.

"I figured I might as well leave here not regretting anything," Clark said. "And that's how I'm leaving."

Despite Clark's disappointment, it was one of the greatest days in US Olympic snowboarding history. The dominance of the US women's team in the halfpipe came one day after the US men also took gold, silver, and fourth place.

"[The Americans] have really good conditions, good pipes, good weather [in the United Sates]," said Norway's Kjersti Buaas, who won the

US snowboarders, *from left*, Hannah Teter, Kelly Clark, and Gretchen Bleiler pose for a photo before the 2006 Olympic halfpipe finals.

bronze medal, just ahead of Clark. "We've got to go there and practice. They're a little bit ahead of us."

Having Fun

Bleiler was the favorite going into the 2006 Olympics. She rode really well during Grand Prix competitions in the weeks leading up to the Games. Bleiler was great during the Olympics, too. Her silver-medal-winning run netted a score of 43.4 points.

Teter, meanwhile, had been a little shaky going into the finals. Her knee bothered her a bit during the Games. Her training had been inconsistent. On the day of competition, though, Teter was ready to go.

"She had that bounce," said Amen Teter, Hannah's brother. "She was having fun, and when Hannah's having fun, she's riding her best."

Teter certainly had fun in the moments before her final ride. She had fun during the ride. And she had fun after the ride.

"Coming in today, I could feel it, being caught up with the energy and the emotion of the whole scene here," Teter said.

Teter became a star. Fans loved her because she won. But they also were drawn to her fun-loving personality. Of course, how could fans not like a girl who carried her own homemade syrup with her? Growing up in

Still Strong

Team USA had plenty of experience in the women's halfpipe heading into the 2010 Olympic Winter Games in Vancouver, Canada. Kelly Clark had won the gold medal in 2002. Hannah Teter had won the gold in 2006. Both went for the gold again in 2010. Instead, the competition belonged to Australia's Torah Bright. She took the gold with an impressive performance. Teter and Clark made the United States proud again, though. Teter won the silver medal and Clark took home the bronze. That gave Team USA six of the 12 medals awarded in the women's halfpipe from 1998 to 2010.

Hannah Teter soars above the village during her gold-medal-winning halfpipe run at the 2006 Olympic Winter Games.

a small town of Vermont, Teter and her brother learned how to climb trees and collect sap in buckets. They would collect the sap and turn it into maple syrup.

"Our syrup is the bomb," Teter said.

On that February day in Turin, however, it was Teter who was the bomb. She soared high above the competition. And with her leading the way, the United States proved once again that it was the strongest country in the world in the halfpipe.

6

Vancouver 2010
WESCOTT REPEATS

There were a lot of questions about Seth Wescott heading into the 2010 Olympic Winter Games in Vancouver, Canada. The American had won the first Olympic men's snowboard cross gold medal in 2006 in Turin, Italy. He hoped to defend that gold medal in 2010. But going into the Vancouver Games, Wescott had not been at his best. There were other riders during World Cup events that looked better than Wescott. The World Cup is a series of high-level international competitions.

American Seth Wescott, *left*, races down the hill during the snowboard cross competition at the 2010 Olympic Winter Games in Vancouver, Canada.

Despite those disappointing World Cup results, Wescott came into Vancouver confident. He was so confident, in fact, that he handed a United States flag to a media relations officer and told her, "I'm going to need this at the finish."

Racing to First

Snowboard cross is known for its unpredictability. Riders must be fast and skilled snowboarders. But perhaps just as important, they also have to be lucky. Racing down a mountain with jumps and curves—not to mention other riders—can result in unexpected crashes. That is part of what makes the sport so exciting.

Wescott got off to a slow start in Vancouver. He was seventeenth in the qualifying rounds. That put him fourth among Americans. Then he hit his stride.

Swiss Siblings

Team USA has had the most success in Olympic snowboarding through 2014. The next-best country has been Switzerland. One of the best moments for the Swiss came at the 2006 Olympic Winter Games in Turin, Italy. Philipp Schoch won the men's parallel giant slalom. That made him the first two-time gold-medal winner in snowboarding. What made it even more special, though, was that he raced his brother, Simon, in the finals. Simon won the silver. "We knew that we could do it," Simon said. "It's actually a dream come true."

Each round of elimination, from the first round to the finals, features four racers competing against each other. The top two in each heat advance to the next round.

After his poor performance in the qualifying rounds, Wescott placed first in his heat in the opening round. Then he won his quarterfinal heat. And after that, he finished second in his semifinal heat. Now he was just one win away from successfully defending his gold medal.

In the finals, Wescott did not get off to a good start. He was in fourth place during the first half of the race. He then moved into third when teammate Nate Holland slipped on the fourth turn. That slip cost Holland a medal. He finished fourth.

Moments after he passed Holland, Wescott zipped past France's Tony Ramoin. Now his sights were set on the leader, Canada's Mike Robertson. The home favorite, Robertson had a sizeable lead. But Wescott was aggressive going into the final jumps and turns. He slipped by Robertson and then held him off down the stretch.

"Pressure situations like this kick me into a different level of motivation," Wescott said. "It's an amazing feeling to have a singular goal all season and accomplish that goal."

Special Flag

As for that flag, it had special meaning. It wasn't just a symbol of his confidence. It was a tribute to his late grandfather, Ben Wescott. His grandfather was a veteran of World War II. The flag had been draped on Ben Wescott's coffin before he was buried.

"My grandfather was a trainer in the army," Wescott said. "He trained troops in World War II. [The flag] has got all the meaning in the world to me."

The world saw that flag in 2006, too. After Wescott won the gold medal in Turin, his father, Jim, jumped over security barriers to wrap the flag around Seth. This time, Seth brought the flag himself. But Jim and Seth's mom, Margaret, were there at the finish line again.

Unlucky

Lindsey Jacobellis is arguably the best snowboard cross rider in the world. Through 2014, she had eight Winter X Games gold medals and three world titles. But her experience at her three Olympics highlighted the unpredictable nature of her sport. In 2006, Jacobellis, then 20, was in the lead and just a few seconds away from a gold medal. That's when, two jumps from the finish, she tried to show off with a grab of her board. She fell, however. Switzerland's Tanja Frieden passed her at the finish line. Jacobellis settled for silver. In 2010 and 2014, she again was a favorite. But she failed to advance from the semifinals both times.

Seth Wescott celebrates after crossing the finish line just ahead of Canada's Mike Robertson, *left*, to win the 2010 Olympic snowboard cross gold medal.

"When Seth has a big race, I don't talk to him all week," Jim said. "I think he turns his cell phone off, doesn't check his email. He needs to be in his own zone. So this was the first time I saw him. I just hugged him and told him I loved him."

Sochi 2014
SLOPESTYLE
DEBUTS

Sage Kotsenburg has never been too far away from the snow. He grew up in Park City, Utah. Many events at the 2002 Olympic Winter Games were held there. It is home to some of the best ski and snowboard trails in the United States. Kotsenburg first got on a snowboard when he was five years old, and he was hooked.

By the time he was 16, in 2010, Kotsenburg had made a name for himself in the snowboarding world. That year, he won a silver medal at X Games Europe in

American Sage Kotsenburg performs a trick during his final run in men's slopestyle at the 2014 Olympic Winter Games in Sochi, Russia.

the slopestyle event. For slopestyle snowboarders like Kotsenburg, the X Games was the most important event. However, the IOC announced in the summer of 2011 that men's and women's slopestyle snowboarding would be added to the Olympics. The sport would make its Olympic debut at the 2014 Winter Games in Sochi, Russia. That gave Kotsenburg and other slopestyle racers a new goal to push for.

At age 20 in 2014, Kotsenburg achieved his goal. He was selected to compete for Team USA in the first Olympic slopestyle competition. Although Kotsenburg was headed to Sochi, few expected him to win anything. Teammate Shaun White was considered to be the top US contender for gold. Even when White withdrew from the competition,

Parallel Slalom Debuts

Slopestyle wasn't the only event to debut during the 2014 Olympic Winter Games. Parallel slalom was also contested for the first time. Parallel slalom is a shorter version of the parallel giant slalom, which has been contested since 2002. Russia's Vic Wild won the men's gold medal. He also won the gold medal in the parallel giant slalom. That made him the first snowboarder to win two gold medals in the same Olympics. Wild was actually born in White Salmon, Washington. In 2011, he married Alena Zavarzina, a Russian snowboarder, and he became a Russian citizen. Austria's Julia Dujmovits won the women's gold medal. Team USA did not win any medals in the parallel slalom.

however, Kotsenburg wasn't viewed as a favorite. Canadians Mark McMorris and Max Parrot were seen as the riders to beat.

Kotsenburg posted a score of 86.50 in the qualifying round. Eleven athletes had better scores. The top eight finishers moved on to the finals. Kotsenburg had to go on to the semifinal round. But the US rider rallied to finish second in the semifinals and advance. Then, in the finals, he shined.

Going for It

Just a few minutes before the finals began, Kotsenburg decided to add a new trick to his run. He successfully landed a backside 1620 with a Japan grab. He called the trick the Holy Crail.

"I had never, ever tried that trick I landed on the last jump," he said. "I went down and winged it and landed it first try, pretty much perfect. I could have got it a little bit better, I think, but it was a never-been-done-before trick."

Landing that trick led Kotsenburg to a sensational score of 93.5 points out of 100. Still, he was just the third rider out of 12 to compete. So he had to wait for nine others to complete the first run—and then wait through the entire second run.

"I was on pins and needles the whole time watching the event," he said. "It was miserable. Honestly, today in slopestyle, [McMorris or

Team USA's Sage Kotsenburg performs a grab during the slopestyle finals at the 2014 Olympic Winter Games.

Norway's Stale Sandbech] any day of the week could have won. There [were] about five runs that I watched them come down and was like, 'I'm done. I'm definitely not getting gold.'"

He did, though. None of the other competitors could top what Kotsenburg did on his first run. He walked away with the first Olympic gold medal in his event's history

"It's pretty crazy," he said. "It all seems so unreal right now."

Jamie Anderson Matches Up

The women hit the mountain one day after the men. And again it was Team USA making history. Jamie Anderson, who grew up in South Lake Tahoe, California, took home the first gold medal in women's slopestyle.

Unlike Kotsenburg, Anderson went into the event as the favorite. She didn't disappoint, either. Anderson had the second-best score during the qualifying round. Then, in the final, she blew everybody away with her score of 95.25 points. Brushing aside her fear of heights, Anderson flew through the air with near perfection. She landed two 720 jumps in her amazing run.

The gold medal wasn't secured until the very end, though. On her first run of the finals, she scored just 80.75 points. She had to wait until the very end of the second round to have her gold-medal moment.

Bacon Medal

After winning his gold medal during the 2014 Olympics in Sochi, Russia, Sage Kotsenburg went to Twitter and wrote, "Ahh I wish the Sochi medals were made out of bacon thoooo..!!" A few days later, Kotsenburg appeared on Conan O'Brien's late-night talk show. During the interview, O'Brien presented Kotsenburg with a medal made out of bacon. Kotsenburg, of course, ate the bacon medal.

US snowboarder Jamie Anderson performs a trick during the slopestyle finals at the 2014 Olympic Winter Games. She won the gold medal.

Finland's Enni Rukajarvi held the lead. Anderson was a distant fifth. But on that final run, Anderson left no doubt who the true champion was.

"Jamie's an awesome competitor," said teammate Karly Shorr, who finished sixth. "She does whatever she has to [in order to] win. She never cracks under pressure. She uses it. She lands."

In 2014, slopestyle snowboarding landed in the Olympics. Kotsenburg and Anderson made it a memorable beginning.

"I think most of us have been thinking about this for a few years," Anderson said. "To just have that moment come so quick and really knowing this is your moment, you just want to shine and do your best and show the world what a fun sport snowboarding is."

Sochi 2014
A US SURPRISE

T he US women had traditionally starred in the Olympic halfpipe. And many people predicted that an American would wind up with the gold medal at the 2014 Olympic Winter Games in Sochi, Russia. After all, Kelly Clark had won the gold in 2002. She was performing better than anyone in the world going into the 2014 Winter Games. Hannah Teter, the 2006 gold medalist, was expected to find herself at or near the top of the podium, too. Up-and-comer Arielle Gold was the defending world champion. Then, of course, there

Few expected Kaitlyn Farrington to win the halfpipe gold medal going into the 2014 Olympic Winter Games in Sochi, Russia.

was 2010 gold medalist Torah Bright from Australia. If one of the top Americans wasn't going to win, surely Bright was going to.

In the end, though, it was a lesser-known American who beat all the champs.

Kaitlyn Farrington, a 24-year-old from Idaho, stunned everybody by winning the gold medal in Sochi. Bright won silver, Clark won the bronze, and Teter finished fourth. Farrington said she came into the Winter Games confident. But afterward she admitted, "I don't think I knew I was going to come here and get a gold medal. I still don't really believe it."

The gold-medal-winning run came early in the second round of the finals. Farrington scored 91.75 points. Her run included a difficult combination of a backside 720 into a backside 900. It was a great run.

Make It Three

Snowboarding has consistently grown since its Olympic debut in 1998. After having just two snowboarding events in 1998 and 2002, the Olympic program added snowboard cross in 2006. Then parallel slalom and slopestyle were added to the program in 2014. Australian star Torah Bright made history by qualifying to compete in three of the five events in 2014. Her best event was halfpipe. Four years after winning Olympic gold, Bright took the silver medal in 2014. She also took seventh place in the debut of Olympic slopestyle snowboarding. In addition, Bright reached the quarterfinals in snowboard cross.

But with three former gold-medal winners still ready to ride, Farrington hardly felt comfortable atop the leaderboard.

Then, one by one, the favorites came up short. Farrington joined the others as an Olympic champion. For Farrington and her family, it was the ultimate reward for a long journey.

Selling the Cows

Farrington grew up as a cowgirl on a ranch in Idaho. As she got better in snowboarding, her parents had to make a difficult decision. They started selling off some of their cattle to pay for her to train and compete around the world.

Farrington began seeing great results as a teenager. She won a silver medal at the 2008 Junior World Championships. She was the 2010 Dew Tour overall champ. She also won a gold medal at the 2010 Winter X Games. Farrington kept getting better, and eventually the family sold all of the cattle.

"I'm sure they do not miss those cows today," Farrington said after winning the gold.

Farrington barely made the US team for Sochi. She earned the final spot just a few weeks before the Olympics began.

"It took me about a week to sink in that I had qualified for the team, because we went to X Games right after, so it was all just so fast," she said. "I kind of believed it when I was on my flight to Sochi, and now to leave as a gold medalist, I'm just beside myself about it."

Once she arrived in Sochi, Farrington took the long road to the gold medal. The top three scorers in each qualifying heat advanced to the finals. Bright, Clark, and Teter all reached the finals with ease. Farrington, however, was one of the 12 competitors who had to then go through a semifinal round. She then was the top finisher in the semifinals. But she still had to take on the champs in the finals.

Parallel Giant Slalom Woes

Since 2002, the United States has dominated the halfpipe competitions at the Olympic Winter Games. The parallel giant slalom discipline was another story, though. From 2002 to 2014, a total of 24 medals were awarded in the parallel giant slalom. Twelve were for women, and 12 were for men. Of those 24, US riders claimed just two. Chris Klug won the first. He took bronze in the men's event at the 2002 Olympic Winter Games. Klug was actually the only American male to make it past the first round of elimination from 2002 to 2014. In 2006, Rosey Fletcher became the only US woman to win a medal in the parallel giant slalom. She took home the bronze medal. Fletcher was one of just two US women from 2002 to 2014 to get past the first round. She was the only one to get into the semifinals.

Gold medalist Kaitlyn Farrington, *center*, silver medalist Torah Bright, *left*, and bronze medalist Kelly Clark celebrate after the 2014 Olympic halfpipe competition.

Competing on the biggest stage of her life, Farrington proved she was a champion, too. Her victory gave Team USA three of the five gold medals in Olympic women's halfpipe history. When it was over, Farrington knew exactly how to celebrate.

"I'm going to dance my face off," she said.

Great
Olympians

Jamie Anderson (USA)

At 23, she won the gold medal in the Olympic debut of slopestyle in 2014.

Torah Bright (Australia)

Bright won the women's halfpipe gold in 2010 and the silver in 2014. She competed in a record three snowboarding events in 2014.

Kelly Clark (USA)

The owner of more Olympic medals than any other snowboarder, she won the women's halfpipe in 2002 and took home bronze in 2010 and 2014.

Danny Kass (USA)

Kass won a pair of silver medals for Team USA in the men's halfpipe in 2002 and 2006.

Ross Powers (USA)

Team USA's first Olympic snowboarding medal winner took home bronze in the men's halfpipe in 1998. He then won gold in that event in 2002.

Philipp Schoch (Switzerland)

One of only three snowboarders to repeat as Olympic champion, he won gold in the parallel giant slalom in 2002 and 2006.

Hannah Teter (USA)

She won gold in halfpipe in 2006 and silver in 2010 before finishing fourth in 2014.

Seth Wescott (USA)

A repeat champion in the snowboard cross, Wescott won gold in 2006 and 2010.

Shaun White (USA)

White won the halfpipe gold medal in 2006, and then did it again in 2010 before finishing fourth in 2014.

Vic Wild (Russia)

The US-born Wild became the first snowboarder to win two gold medals in the same Games, placing first in the parallel giant slalom and the parallel slalom in 2014.

Glossary

ALPINE SKIING

Downhill skiing; the boots are fastened to the ski on both ends.

AMPLITUDE

Great height.

CAB CORK-720

This is a trick that includes a frontside spin (cab) with two rotations (720 degrees). The cork refers to the spin rotating up and down, as well as to the left or right.

CHUTE

A lane through which a snowboarder passes at the start of their run down the mountain.

HALFPIPE

A course built into the snow that is shaped like the letter U. Snowboarders ride up the tall, vertical walls to do tricks.

HEAT

A round of qualifying competition.

JAPAN GRAB

A trick where the athlete pulls the board up behind his or her back.

McTWIST

A jump that includes an inverted backside 540 (one and a half rotations) while the athlete grabs the toe side of the snowboard.

NORDIC SKIING

A type of skiing in which only the front of the boot is connected to the ski. Cross-country skiing and ski jumping are types of Nordic skiing.

SLALOM

A race over a winding mountain course marked by flags.

SLOPESTYLE

A snowboarding competition in which the rider performs tricks on ramps, rails, jumps, and other obstacles.

For More Information

SELECTED BIBLIOGRAPHY

Burns, Kylie. *Winter Olympic Sports: Alpine and Freestyle Skiing*. New York: Crabtree Pub. Co., 2009.

Hunter, Nick. *The Winter Olympics*. London, UK: Heinemann, 2013.

Wukovits, John F. *The Encyclopedia of the Winter Olympics*. New York: Franklin Watts, 2001.

FURTHER READINGS

Judd, Ron C. *The Winter Olympics: An Insider's Guide to the Legends, the Lore, and the Games: Vancouver Edition*. Seattle, WA : Mountaineers Books, 2009.

Teter, Hannah, and Tawnya Schultz. *Mastering Snowboarding*. Champaign, IL: Human Kinetics, 2013.

Wallechinsky, David, and Jaime Loucky. *The Complete Book of the Winter Olympics: 2010 Edition*. London, UK: Aurum Press, 2009.

WEBSITES

To learn more about Great Moments in Olympic Sports, visit **booklinks.abdopublishing.com**. These links are routinely monitored and updated to provide the most current information available.

PLACES TO VISIT

US Olympic Training Center
1750 E Boulder St.
Colorado Springs, CO 80909
(719) 866-4618
www.teamusa.org
The US Olympic team has welcomed more than 1.6 million visitors to its headquarters in Colorado Springs, Colorado. In addition to extensive training facilities for elite athletes, the USOTC offers visitors the chance to discover US Olympic history through its indoor and outdoor exhibitions and installations. Walking tours are conducted daily.

US Ski and Snowboard Hall of Fame and Museum
610 Palms Ave.
Ishpeming, MI 49849
(906) 485-6323
www.skihall.com
The birthplace of organized skiing in the United States. It contains displays and exhibits with countless artifacts relating to the history of skiing and snowboarding.

Index

ABOUT THE AUTHOR

Brian Howell is a freelance writer based in Denver, Colorado. He has been a sports journalist for nearly 20 years, writing about high school, college, and professional athletics. In addition, he has written books about sports and history. A native of Colorado, he lives with his wife and four children in his home state.